A Compilation of Inspirational Quotes

RACHAEL HOWELL

BOOKSIDE Press

Copyright © 2023 by Rachael Howell

ISBN: 978-1-77883-213-0 (Paperback)

          978-1-77883-215-4 (Hardback)

          978-1-77883-214-7 (E-book)

All rights reserved. No part of this publication may be reproduced, distributed, or transmitted in any form or by any means, including photocopying, recording, or other electronic or mechanical methods, without the prior written permission of the publisher, except in the case brief quotations embodied in critical reviews and other noncommercial uses permitted by copyright law.

The views expressed in this book are solely those of the author and do not necessarily reflect the views of the publisher, and the publisher hereby disclaims any responsibility for them.

BookSide Press
877-741-8091
www.booksidepress.com
orders@booksidepress.com

Contents

Introduction v

Success 1

Forgiveness 11

Contentment 17

Knowledge 21

Loving Kindness 25

The Power of Words 31

Relationship 43

Discussion 47

Conclusion 49

Acknowledgment 51

About the Author 53

Introduction

I love quotes and whenever I would read a quote or see and hear a quote I would write it down. One day I said I should put these quotes into a book.

My husband encouraged me to do so. This is teamwork because it is everyone's quote.

Most authors are unknown but their words will encourage, direct, uplift, and bring out the best in everyone.

I am hoping that this compilation of words called quotes will inspire all who read this book, especially young people.

Success

Success is the progressive realization of a worthwhile dream. The true measure of success is the number of obstacles we overcome.
Whatever you do, success or failure is up to you.
Anything the mind of man can conceive and believe it can achieve.

- **Napoleon Hill**

* * * * * *

If you refuse to accept anything but the very best, you usually get it.
Winners don't blame fate for their failures or luck for their successes.
When we teach others we are not just spending time, we are investing it.
Believe in yourself, do not let your limitations hold you back.
Do not make the color of your skin or your body weight determine your success.
It is not always those with the longest drive who win the game; It is those who have the drive and determination to stay the course.

- **Unknown**

Good better best, never let it rest until your good is better and your better best.

— **St. Jerome**

In other words: Never stop trying until you become the best you can be.

* * * * *

Teamwork lessens the task and multiplies the success.

— **Unknown**

In other words: You can accomplish more when working together than when working alone.

* * * * *

What one man imagines, another man can make real.

— **Jules Verne**

* * * * *

Never look down on anyone unless you are helping him up.

— **Jesse Jackson**

* * * * *

The greatest service you can render someone else is helping him help himself.

                                                    - Unknown

In other words: If you teach someone how to help himself, you do not have to help him for the rest of his life.

* * * * *

Courage is not having the strength to go on, it is going on when you do not have the strength.

                                                    - Unknown

* * * * *

Age may wrinkle the skin, but to give up interest wrinkles the soul.

                                                    - Douglas McArthur

* * * * *

Stop doing permanent things with temporary people.

                                                    - Unknown

* * * * *

It is not always those with the longest drive who win the game; it is those who have the drive and determination to stay the course.

— **Unknown**

* * * * *

How we prepare for tomorrow depends on how we use today.

— **Unknown**

* * * * *

You are never too old to set a new goal or to dream a new dream.

— **Unknown**

* * * * *

The only people who fail are those who do not try.

— **Unknown**

* * * * *

Failure to prepare is preparing to fail
It is better to try and fail than to fail to try.
With God all things are possible.
$$\text{Mark 10:27}$$

* * * * *

Wisdom resteth in the heart of him that hath understanding.
$$\text{Proverbs 14:33}$$

* * * * *

Encouraging the young should never become old.
$$\text{- \textbf{Unknown}}$$

In other words: Never stop giving the young encouraging words.
* * * * *

To earn tomorrow, you have to learn today.
$$\text{- \textbf{Slinger Francisco}}$$

* * * * *

Learn as if to live forever; live as if to die today.
>   — **Mahatma Gandhi**

*****

He who laughs last laughs best.
>   — **Unknown**

*****

Heights that great men reached and kept were not attained by sudden flight; but they while their companions slept, were toiling upwards in the night.
>   — **Henry Wadsworth Longfellow**

*****

"Strong minds discuss ideas. Average minds discuss events. Weak minds discuss people."
>   — **Socrates**

*****

He who knows not and knows that he knows not is a child, teach him.
He who knows and knows not that he knows is asleep, wake him.
He who knows not, and knows not that he knows not, is a fool shone on him.
He who knows and knows that he knows is wise, follow him.
— **Unknown**

* * * * *

You may give without loving, but you cannot love without giving.
— **Unknown**

* * * * *

Forgiveness

Forgiveness is greater than anger and compassion is more powerful than vengeance.

- The Bible

* * * * *

Without forgiveness the potential for true happiness in one's life is limited.

- Unknown

* * * * *

Always forgive others not because they deserve forgiveness; but because you deserve peace of mind.

- Unknown

In other words: If you do not forgive, you will become more miserable than the one who did you wrong.

* * * * *

As light overcomes darkness, goodness can overcome evil.

- The Bible

* * * * *

Revenge imprisoned us, forgiveness set us free.
- **Unknown**

* * * * *

Conduct is the best proof of character.
- **Unknown**

* * * * *

Unity among believers comes from our union with Christ.
- **Unknown**

* * * * *

Whether our sins are great or small, Jesus is able to forgive them all.
- **The Bible**

* * * * *

A soft answer turneth away wrath but grievous words stir up anger.

- The Bible

* * * * *

Returning good for good is human, returning good for evil is divine.

- The Bible

* * * * *

A caring word can accomplish more than we can ever imagine.

- Unknown

* * * * *

Those who reward evil for good, evil shall not depart from their house.

- The Bible

* * * * *

Sticks and stones can break your bones but harsh words linger longer.

— **Unknown**

* * * * *

Whether morning, noon, or night, make God's word you delight.

— **Unknown**

* * * * *

Conduct is the best proof of character.

— **Unknown**

* * * * *

There is hope with God even in the most hopeless situation.
						- The Bible

* * * * *

Being all fashioned of the self-same dust, let us be merciful as well as just.
						- The Bible

* * * * *

Contentment

Contentment is not possessing everything, but giving thanks for everything that you possess.

— **Unknown**

* * * * *

When you are content you learn to accept the bitter with the sweet.

— **Unknown**

* * * * *

He is rich who is satisfied with what he has.

— **Unknown**

* * * * *

God blesses us so that we can bless others.

— **The Bible**

* * * * *

He that shares his wealth with the poor shall be blessed.
- **Proverbs**

* * * * *

Discontentment makes rich people poor, while contentment makes poor people rich.
- **Unknown**

* * * * *

Dear God, if I can't have what I want! Let me want what I have.
- **Unknown**

* * * * *

It is better to get wisdom than gold and to choose understanding than silver.
- **Proverbs**

* * * * *

No matter who signs your paycheck, you are really working for God.

- **Unknown**

* * * * *

Knowledge

A natural feeling of mankind is the desire to acquire knowledge.

— **Unknown**

* * * * *

Knowledge is power.

— **Francis Bacon**

* * * * *

Not only is there an art in knowing a thing but also a certain art in teaching it.

— **Marcus Tullius Cicero**

* * * * *

To know is not to know unless someone else has known that you know.

— **Lucillus**

* * * * *

He that hath understanding seeketh Knowledge; but the mouth of fools feedeth on foolishness.

               - Proverbs

*****

He who walks with the wise will be wise; he who walks with the fool will be foolish.

               - Proverbs

*****

Who can direct, when all pretend to know?

               - Goldsmith

*****

Growing up is optional, growing old is mandatory.

               - Walt Disney

In other words: As long as you remain alive you will grow old.

*****

If we bury the mistakes of the past we are destined to relive them in the future.

— **Unknown**

*****

In other words: If we learn from our mistakes it is possible we will not repeat them.

Loving Kindness

Kindness picks others up when troubles weigh them down. Pleasant words are as sweet to the soul and healthy to the bones.
Praise loudly and correct softly.

            - Unknown

* * * * *

The glory of life is to love, not to be loved; to give, not to get; to serve, not to be served.

           - John Templeton

* * * * *

It is nice to be important, but it is more important to be nice. The seeds we sow today determine the kind of fruit we will reap tomorrow.

            - The Bible

* * * * *

The key to getting along with others is having the mind of Christ.

- The Bible

* * * * *

Real love is helping others, even if they can never return the favor.
Failure to discipline our children is a failure to love them.
We make a living by what we get, we make a life by what we give.

- Unknown

* * * * *

We learn from our mistakes. God's love does not keep us from trials; but sees us through them.

- Unknown

* * * * *

Whoever guards his mouth and tongue keeps his soul from troubles.

- **Proverb**

*****

A word of encouragement can make the difference between giving up or going on.

- **Unknown**

*****

Affection plus correction leads to direction. God's love in our hearts gives us a heart for others. Words spoken rashly do more harm than good.

- **The Bible**

*****

The sound of an encouraging word gives hope to the human spirit.

- **Proverb**

*****

The joy of living comes from a heart of thanksgiving.
If you are tempted to lose patience with another, stop and think how patient God has been with you.
Our words have the power to build up or to tear down.

              - The Bible

* * * * *

The words of a talebearer are as wounds and they go down into the innermost parts of the belly.

              - Proverb

* * * * *

True listening is not just hearing words, it is receiving and understanding the message.

              - Unknown

* * * * *

The one is truely wise who gains his wisdom from the experience of others.

              - Unknown

* * * * *

GOD work in us to grow us into what he wants us to be.
— **The Bible**

* * * * *

Hatred promotes self-destruction, love fulfills Christ's instruction.
— **Unknown**

* * * * *

If you tell the truth you do not have to remember anything. The love of God motivates us to live for God.
— **The Bible.**

* * * * *

The Power of Words

Life and death is in the power of the tongue.

- **The Bible**

* * * * *

It is not what you do every once in a while; but what you dedicate yourself to on a daily basis that makes a difference.

- **Unknown**

* * * * *

Never let what other people expect from you dictate what you expect from yourself.

- **Unknown**

* * * * *

Wake up each morning determined, so you can go to bed satisfied.

- **Unknown**

* * * * *

Life may not be the party we hoped for, but while we are here we might as well dance.

— **Unknown**

In other words: Be content with your life.

* * * * *

Let him who thinks he stands, take heed lest he fall.

— **Proverb**

* * * * *

The pen is mightier than the sword.

— **Edward Buliver-Lytton**

* * * * *

Trials reveal our character.

— **James Lane Allen**

* * * * *

A debt is never too old for an honest person to pay.

— **Unknown**

*****

Don't let the noise of the world keep you from hearing the voice of the Lord.

- Unknown

*****

To be found, you must first admit that you are lost.

- Unknown

*****

There is none more blind than those who fail to see.
You do not stop playing because you grow old; you grow old because you stop playing.

- Unknown

In other words: As long as you are breathing the breath of life you are going to grow old whether you like it or not.
*****

When troubles call on you, call on God.

- The Bible

*****

Speech is silver but silence is gold.
In other words: If you do not have anything good to say keep silent.

*****

People forget how fast you did a job but they remember how well you did it.
- **Unknown**

*****

The true test of our character is what we do when no one is watching.
- **John Wooden**

*****

United we stand, divided we fall.
- **John Dickinson**

*****

Let us never negotiate out of fear, but let us never fail to negotiate.

            - John F Kennedy

* * * * *

When God says no to our request, we can be sure it is for the best.

                - The Bible

* * * * *

He who laughs last, laughs best.

                 - Unknown

* * * * *

Loneliness is a terrible price to pay for independence.

                 - Unknown

* * * * *

No sorrow is too heavy for our Savior to bear.

Bad men live that they may eat and drink, whereas good men eat and drink that they may live.

– **Socrates.**

* * * * *

When you come to the Lord, there is no waiting line; his ears are always open to your cry.

– **Unknown**

* * * * *

Hell and destruction are never full so the eyes of man are never satisfied.

– **Proverbs**

* * * * *

All the labor of man is for his mouth, and yet the appetite is not filled.

– **Ecclesiastes 6:7**

* * * * *

Nothing can fill the emptiness in your heart except God.
- **The Bible**

* * * * *

You are confined only by the walls you build yourself.
- **Andrew Murphy**

* * * * *

We must all suffer from one or two pains, the pain of discipline or the pain of regret; the difference is discipline weighs ounces, while regret weighs tons.
- **Jim Rohn**

In other words: If we fail to discipline our children we will contribute to their downfall.

* * * * *

Keep praising God from whom all blessings flow.
- **The Bible**

* * * * *

A sunset in one land is a sunrise in another.
- **Unknown**

* * * * *

In other words: Weeping may endure for a night but joy comes in the morning Psalms.

* * * * *

When temptations knock at your door, don't ask them in for lunch.

- Unknown

In other words: When you yield to temptation you will end up in a lot of trouble.

* * * * *

Do not stop to stone the devil's dog or he might turn around and bite you.

In other words: If you go around looking for trouble it may just find you.

* * * * *

What we think is what we become.

- Proverbs 23:7

* * * * *

Life matters, make the most of it.

- Unknown

In other words: Enjoy your life because we do not know how long we have to live on this earth.

* * * * *

When the world around you is crumbling, God is the rock on which you can stand.

- The Bible

* * * * *

No one can drive you crazy unless you give them the keys.
- Mike Bechtle

* * * * *

Righteousness exalteth a nation but sin is a reproach to any people.

- The Bible

* * * * *

In other words: The Nation that puts God first is blessed. Our greatest comfort in sorrow is to know that God is in control at all times.

- The Bible

* * * * *

A merry heart maketh a cheerful countenance; but by sorrow of the heart, the spirit is broken.

- Proverbs 15:13

* * * * *

Do not make circumstances suck all the joy out of your life; you have to make the decision to be happy.
In other words: No one can make you happy; Happiness comes from within.

* * * * *

True peace comes from the prince of peace.
Life's greatest joy is the sure hope of heaven.
Let God's word fill your memory, rule your heart and guide your life.

* * * * *

Relationship

The most important ingredients of any long-lasting relationship are mutual respect, understanding, tolerance, and patience.

- **Unknown**

* * * * *

Love is not genuine until it has been shared.

- **Unknown**

* * * * *

In order for one to be successful in marriage. It's not finding the right person, it is being the right person.

- **Unknown**

* * * * *

Pride leads to destruction and arrogance to downfall.

- **Proverbs**

* * * * *

In other words: Be humble, let someone else praise you instead of you praising yourself.
Jealousy is as cruel as the grave.
- **The Bible**

In other words: Some people would kill to get what belongs to another.
* * * * *

The remedy for jealousy is thankfulness to God.
- **Unknown**

In other words: If we are thankful to God for what we have; we would not be envious of other people's possessions.

* * * * *

Discussion

For most of my life, I wanted to write a book. I did not want to write fiction or anyone's life story.

Year after year I would voice my desire to my friends and co-workers about writing a book. Many years passed, and then I met a co-worker who said to me "Did you write that book as yet?" The thought came alive again and I began to think what I would write.

Conclusion

Young people who did not grow up around elderly folks may not be aware of most of these quotes.

These quotes make you think about yourselves, the life you want to live, the heights you can reach, and the love you can share.

Furthermore, reading these quotes may change your outlook on life and toward others.

Acknowledgment

I am deeply grateful to my husband for his patience and encouragement as always; more so since I began to put these quotes together.

To my lovely daughter who encourages me to compile these quotes and sees them as words to live by.

Last but not least, to my son who gave me valuable advice while I was writing this project.

About the Author

Rachael Howell was born on the beautiful West Indian Island of Antigua to Susanah Daniel and Daniel Green. She was the fifth of twelve children. At the age of nine years, she knew that she wanted to become a Nurse to help the sick to recover. After graduating from High School she applied and was accepted into the Nursing program. Four years later she became a Registered nurse. She met Victor Howell and after dating for two years and nine months, they came together in Holy Matrimony. From that union came two children, Carlon and Randez Howell. Rachael and Victor have a very loving and supportive relationship and are still very much in love after forty-one years of marriage.

In 1982 the family migrated to the United States Virgin Island of St Croix where they resided for six years. Rachael worked in the Government Hospital there. In 1989 her family relocated to New Jersey and is now residing in the Township of Maplewood.

For many years Rachael thought about writing a book. She would voice her desire to friends and family members.

She also liked to read quotes since she was in High School and she would share them to those who were willing to listen. She never dismissed the thought of writing a book. Four years ago the thought came to her to compile a book of inspirational quotes. Rachael likes to listen to religious music. She plays the piano, and practices the guitar and the harmonica; not good at those. She puts the Almighty God first in everything that she does. He is her all in all. Her hobbies are reading and traveling. European countries are her favorite places to visit. Places visited outside of the USA are Germany, Switzerland, Austria, Hungary, Spain, Portugal, Denmark, Norway, Sweden, Greece, Turkey, Finland, Russia, England, France, Belgium, Holland, Italy, Czechoslovakia, Croatia, Slovakia, Bulgaria, Macedonia, Bosnia, Slovenia, Albania, Montenegro and China. She still travels at least twice a year.

www.ingramcontent.com/pod-product-compliance
Lightning Source LLC
LaVergne TN
LVHW041544060526
838200LV00037B/1133